IN THE WORLD
ENORMOUS

IN THE WORLD ENORMOUS

TOMER INBAR

Station Hill Press
BARRYTOWN, NEW YORK

Published by Station Hill Press, the publishing project of the Institute for Publishing Arts, Inc., 120 Station Hill Road, Barrytown, NY 12507, New York, a not-for-profit, Section 501(c)(3) tax-exempt organization.

Online catalogue: www.stationhill.org
e-mail: publishers@stationhill.org

This publication is supported in part by grants from the New York State Council on the Arts, a state agency.

Cover and interior design by Susan Quasha

Library of Congress Cataloging-in-Publication Data

Names: Inbar, Tomer, author.
Title: In the world enormous / Tomer Inbar.
Description: Barryton, NY : Station Hill Press, [2018]
Identifiers: LCCN 2018023025 | ISBN 9781581771732 (pbk.)
Classification: LCC PS3609.N33 A6 2018 | DDC 813/.6—dc23
LC record available at https://lccn.loc.gov/2018023025

Manufactured in the United States of America

For the memory of my mother & the persistence, support & mischief of all the other Inbars

CONTENTS

I. FIRST

AND A WREN HAS BROUGHT THEM

Pulling twigs & a wren has brought them from a nest
abandoned by a certain bird in a wooden box I am certain
it will return to

Or taking pains to discern the outcome of a discussion
between friends in passing a fountain or a cornfield or the
last building beyond it

So often it is a garden) white linen strips & wraps of wire
mesh delimit (a guard rail bent to shape it (wildflowers on
a hill exaggerated

I find these effective: come what may (pardon the intrusion
(a minute of your time is all I ask) (though a wren has
brought them I am certain the other will return (I have it in
good standing)

This then told while pulling twigs from a nest the one has
left etc. while dressing for dinner or discerning the need for
caution by a light switch in a discussion between friends

(Each has its merits)

Nor do I disallow the pleasure the one has taken to
dismantle what the other has accomplished (nor favor the
first who has abandoned its pleasure) however disinclined
I am to favor the intrusion

For there are twigs in abundance at the foot of a certain
post & cracks in abundance & wind in abundance in the
wood of the walls a small box has

& I recognize in it the actions of either as my own as I seem to favor above all else the disinclination to state simply my pleasure with what the wren has brought

II. CONVERSATIONAL
(MOTHERS & DAUGHTERS

THE LUNCH SPOT

We are unwilling to accept the rain
as it is

I am speaking to myself & a grey
flannel jacket (striped pants (soft
leather boots) on the second floor
of the Lunch Spot (I say to her: we
should gather the clipping (but only
the radiant ones) & note the glances
upward (the trajectory of the wind
& so on

All (she said) to what end (if we are
unwilling (as you say) to accept what
it brings

From the second floor of the Lunch
Spot I say to her: tell me about the
concentric ones (in grey flannel
boots (striped pants leather gloves)
traces of rain & fingertips tracing
the rain in large circles & the smaller
circles beneath them

(as if to brush away this sound would
leave you open to the usual charges
or suggestions to the contrary)

I can see it now (we are the first to
come round & I say (then (to her)

on the second floor of the Lunch
Spot (where we stop often (that the
rain is crowded with grey flannel &
stripes moving towards center (as)
the canals on either side fill & drain
& fill & drain

FROST

Some parts freeze (what frost
does

By evening my mouth is an
open-air tunnel (wet where
the road picks up) &

Some

(like frost) arrive promptly
& some (like melancholy (for
one) simply arrive (willing to
play & then) some

(we

have
not
heard
yet

move

like

(wet flowers
across a red
flower
bed)

one rock to the next

(it is)

to describe
what frost does

only

slower

CINQUE TERRE

(after a line by James Schuyler)

It draws my attention to the other
hand for instance or a temperate
day out of season) at a local shop)
(negotiating the purchase of a long
fence for one that is missing

I stop at the curb where the water
passes & mark the sum of its parts:

RAPID DELIVERY

For the some that keep rushing
by (the usual urgency keeps about
them) as our neighbors make love
before the street lamps go on (it
is what I notice (regularly (that)
resonates (somehow) the way five
towns in the hills of Northern Italy
do (to a point (you say) take up
space on Long Island (Larry grew up
in Laurence (remember) & Lauren in
Cedarhurst & Ruthie in Rockaway
the odd one out) but then (you ask
(is it better to find a way around the
yearly celebrations for the centennial
of a particular bridge (named after a
Polish war hero or the governor of
an inland state (after all (fair is fair
(in all love has to offer & don't get

me started about the directions' lack
of clarity (not to mention how (with
each passing day (I can't remember
(what it was like) when the sun could
place such colors & turn ordinary
monuments on their heads with envy

In the World Enormous

(for Helen Inbar)

In the world enormous (the
bridge is narrow (it alone
is) & the geese (step out of
their canal as after dawn (one
by one (with time to spare.
It is far enough for them
(this world enormous) with
its symmetries & favor this
favor that moments) as our
remains lie still on a shelf in
a room filled with sunlight
(brittle when the touch comes
(though) some will

We are (after all) stepping in
their footsteps (one by one
against our better judgment
(as the natural ones do) we pull
out the stops & remember the
touch of the first one that did
or the certainty one would
return (though it did not (&
for good reason) & to this
we are drawn (the pleasure
(stated simply) is how these
actions choose: twigs from
the mouth of a wren (wind
in the wood of the walls & all
else (likewise) in abundance
between them

BLUE (ROSES. SHIVA

(for my mother)

I.   Dawn (shall stave these)

At dawn the moveable property fills
with cicadas. Women throw candy
& place ashes by the bedside (we are
told (& do) refrain from excessive
lamentation (nor sigh nor weep
nor cutting of flesh) & to recognize
certainty (also) in the good fixtures
(the better fabric (piece by piece) on
lines (stained at places

(& dawn shall stave us their weights
and measures (stiff in places (though
evenly force(d) as lately (is (as is
(cold (as) it is

II.   Blue

They are blue now. The ash blue
bundles & bundles of blue sticks.
Every blue word echoes: (blue rose
blue rose blue roses are red) &
just) barely blue (ash(es) fall(s) like
lightning. (Blue.

III.   Notify

In case of death (please) notify) self.

IV.   Directions

Complete all forms before arrival.
Drop forms in the box to the left of
the gate. The driver does not carry
forms. Keep the directions pinned
to the soft edges behind the mirror.
Crack the window. (Again). Keep
forms (in) certain (places. The closing
doors (for one mind the twigs

the) ovens (are (first to the gate.

V.   What Her Father Would
        Say (About)

What her father would say (about)
the quickest way around the block.
Was i(t)n a Cadillac? The pinochle
was never better t)he(y) would say)
It was her jumping from frame (to
frame) to) facing mountains & turn
on the details (of a bird house (the
pond too) All occupants gone to
(other) parts)

She kept sheets of (note paper (for)
recipes (we know (they came gladly)
& would come again (contrary to
what else (we bring: the joyful burn
of small lights) why (not (side (with
the welcome ones

They leave

one frame (to us (. Return in another.

VI.   After Brecht

Each)

as a river) has its (own) poison &

(a) river to return (to)

& each (river) carries poison to itself
(as the sea)

returns

poison to poison & each to its own
(when) all things welcome

Come

VII.   What was (all) hands

What has (all) hands (has all hands
to walk on) other thoughts include:
it would have made a difference
(irregular though we tend to be (at
least punctual) not that her mother
was (waiting (for the time being (just
so

THE DAY ROUTE

It starts (as it often does) in an
exchange between strangers (once
(though no longer) about the health
of a child (it is good to see you both
again & are there others of equal size
& footing (&) if not can I buy back
what is left

(after all is said & done

In an exchange between strangers
I avoid words like: sonorous or
tympanum & stick to the thought
of a news report about the current
phenomena or how thin her arms
appear beneath a stiff white shirt (as
I pass through the doors a moment
too late

(& the conversations that ensue
between strangers

(& the whys and why nots & what
have yous) of: if I am no longer able
(she says) or: it could be worse (he
replies)

That they touch lightly (you
expected otherwise) as they might in
the hands of someone more skilled

in the giving & taking of ordinary
occurrence (it is no specialty of mine
(you say

Or is it) a function of what appears
in these moments to have already
passed. Light headed & in need of a
rest. Warm water in a metal basin &
the day route just over your shoulder
without notice

SENTIENT WATER(S)

& why the spread of shadows
is sentient without hope for
more (across a white wall)

my child
sleeps next
to (sleeping
dogs)

(& who doesn't
live in)
a tinderbox

(once bitten)

We move simply to the next
matter & the arrangement
of matters to come (weighs
heavily (even then

When all is said (& done) ask
these dogs (why they remain
& how shadows sleep with
sentient waters

the moment we recognize

LET THESE DOGS LIE

(If you) can't feel safe in your own
home (no) or in the home of a
neighbor (no) or in the alley leading
from a broken screen door to the
municipal park system of St. Louis
Missouri (no)

Then let wild dogs lie. Let them
sleep. Let the neighbors feel safe. Let
them hear nothing of substance at
the dinner hour the television hour
the bath hour or the sex hour

(no) not in St. Louis Missouri (no)
not in the alleys of St. Louis Missouri
(no) not in the municipal parks &
front yards of St. Louis Missouri (no)
not through my broken screen door
(no) not only in St. Louis Missouri

where these dogs are wild dogs (not
our dogs (no) & the house dogs &
the show dogs & the dogs for dogs'
sake move with these dogs through
the streets of St. Louis Missouri &
hear what wild dogs hear (no) wild
dogs in all directions

wild dogs

in all directions

MATTERS

We think of matters in the ordinary
course. As matters deserve to (or not
(to) in some ways expect (to) bring

Some (matters) close.

They are tepid (you say: take your
seat to the right of the next available
& begin the process of making
(matter after matter

worse)

coming full circle) on a bus or rail car
(polite conversation & warm hands
above the knee)

& then some

In the ordinary course. Clearly.

PACE

The pace of these negotiations (he:
it is good from among the choices)
(she: & why not something different
for a change) is familiar to us (as
branches shift & light deepens &
shutters draw objects (from head to
knee) about the glass top of a white
table.

Some say & (I have heard it often:
pace yourself in pace yourself out as
the cars pass from pole to pole or

We pace up and down the length
(never mind it goes front to back not
top to bottom) of her. Until all else
is clear

We have days like this (you say): "off
our pace"

our friends likewise.

SIGNS OF THE OLD WEST

They are building again. This time
in either direction of K & 18th street
(in the vicinity of the river (distances
travel well) someone has opened
a hole behind the old forge & the
street is mud & bare patches

& some mornings I catch myself
(charging through this disposition
towards bare spring (seeing things
for the first time always helps) at the
start of something big (not asking
the time (coming down with a cold
(something seasonal no (?) But
(you say) at the top of the stairwell
(after what seems like an hour of
conversation (it is not for this reason
that you stay (but) what catches
you in corners. Thin as her. Almost
translucent. Arms are.

IMPRESSION(S)

No loss is the greater of small
impression(s). As in: (the) rain (is
too small) for example (at each end
of (is it always this way (?) It is. Or
does by morning the good company
improve. Having done what needs
doing (to) the mist breaking in short
breaths (daffodils at their stems).
Now & then I hear the caution in
their voices (the quick step over the
curb & the warning (from him to
her) of a leak in the ceiling where
the window barely closes (& the
sounds travel through the pipes (as
the caution in the wind proceeds.
Impression (is) greater than loss (she
replies) brushing stems from stem to
stem.

EFFORT

In this sense the effort is wasted.

Bend a stick above a dry sewer run
or a manhole cover (extending). As
cars pass and shadows divide into
the sum of their parts.

It could be a draft standing too long
in one place (avoiding obstacles (oh)
& the ceiling tiles (badly in need of
relocation (just say the word) & the
volume needed to simplify & "get on
with it" (the rest will come later.

To place (what) effort (there is) at
the positive ends (they approach
& hesitate (with good reason) for
what it's worth (protect & divide the
flank) & push to tie up (immediately)
before it becomes clearly said.

WITH LIGHT HANDS

The distractions of light hands (are
marked (with benevolence) are they
not) obvious) in the last to bend
(without vines (yet cleared)

Distraction (comes like passengers
(slow to arrive) quiescent when
they do (as when fingers (in familiar
gestures) wander (flesh to nail)
across a counter top or quarry bed
(equally pliant)

On these days (let the easy ones pass
& hope for better starts (& luck to
follow) if the timing is right (at a
minimum) & evening lets its light
hands (lessen) the distance (forward)

THE PROJECTIONIST

Then. If the talk comes. Or a door
jams (late in the day. Why send
shivers) down the first to react
(cautious) in different measures
(she: "The burial mounds are full of
ant hills" or (he: as the smaller ones
gain purchase & the company they
keep rides askew (limbs & shoulders
& trouser breaks flying) (trap (trap
(trap) against the side of a metal
canister (all you notice (in the end)
is that (once) I had the good fortune
to... Or better yet: the leaves are full
of color (the leaves are (say) colorful

BROOKLYN BRIDGE ROAD

If the how of it is in the distance)
would it not be (but) cable work
over and over (rover (?)

Not that a rough estimate would have
it stacked & counted & apportioned
differently (like the pigeons they
keep & planters just watered

It is a matter of fact that along the
battlements we take the archers in
stride (as they sway (so like them) &
align before crossing

(it's not something you plan for)

or remember (often enough) to refer
(to it) as (it was) then (simply: a road
between parked cars) thick stockings
as the thighs alight (watch them take
one for (this & one for the that (of
(it) in the recurrence of (certain)
postures we are (otherwise content
to pass (the rest) along

STILL LIFE WITH BRAID AND ROPE

One thing about reflections: (A)
still life with braid & rope (end
over end (water over flower prints
(laid haphazardly about) what we
should take (you said) is: the long
way out. Not without promise or
reward (even) from this height (the
boundary lines post loss. Certainly.

LIST(ING) BIRDS

Promise (fresh onions (or an entire
field of birds (!) The canals (next)
to others too) some schemes (come
& go) quickly (list the birds you see
(the temporary one (like: jays & tiny
warblers (mention pigeons (at the
back of the water treatment plant
where the (rain) runs full bore at us
(& the birds list)

FROM THE BUS

From the bus. I saw:

Toucans & penguins) an arched
doorway & more.

The bus has long fenders. Grey
(green khaki trousers & deep blue
shirts (like mine) & a smoking jacket
slung low over its hips.

The bus stands on its pilings. The
bus differs from its postings.

There are stray dogs on the bus too.

If the bus could cascade over a rocky
surface (the way its passengers do).

I am awake at night thinking of
buses. I am awake at night.

The precise time the bus arrived
was posted. The ads on the bus are
misleading.

The bus is due for repairs. There is
a pawn shop at the back of the bus.

The bus is looking at me. I look
down.

The bus has hired mercenaries to stand by the fence at night. The wind blows the leaves off the bus. The bus has lines painted on its face.

The bus disappears into the mountains. The bus returns a new man.

Without thinking (the bus turns down a dark alley. The bus has six dollars to its name.

The bus opens its mouth. I keep track of the "r"s in its sentences. I notice (its) syntax.

APPOSITION

As: (A layer of mud (is) uneven)
given the climate & sudden changes
(expectations are slow (taken slowly
in) alternatives. Steady the bough as
the sun shifts (or is it just the trees
(ma'am) in the open) cells proximate
in relation to each other (turn)
for instance & catch me without
warning.

(A) Dir(e)ctio(n): of (Absence)

Take (absence) without (warning.
No) modification(s) or direction.
Approach (as the roots open (whole
days hence) & talk (absence) in
familiar terms (slowly) as (far as the)
whole moon (is concerned) it could
walk the length of its cover). No?

ACCIDENTAL

The scope is not accidental (nor
(entirely) without (consequence)

Each petal divides its spoils) &
shares (in abandon appear freshly
cut (folding things arrayed (not yet
lit

Could we do without the confetti &
languor & cloth streamers crossing
(purpose(fully)

As you say: it means business)
& from the looks of it has value
(enough) to hold in presence what
(to us) seems prudent.

At these hours (not much longer
than many) (apply body pressure
lightly

As how it goes about (being) on its
own two feet (then. As appropriate.

MORTUARY

Taking sticks to the mortuary: wild
Iris (bunches (of fresh tea (mint &)
marjoram (be discreet (she said)
I have neither their leisure nor
cadence) to arrive (in her state)
momentarily. She) does not worry
(these sticks will suffice

By late afternoon the canal will rise
as far west as the Palisades) & then)
all bets (resolve them or not) will be
off)

Only moments later could I
remember (any) (a) way (a) piece of
advice taken from a friend)

I'm sure they are awake (at moments
like this most things (decided already
(decide to keep these things (kept)

Say what you will about recognition
(I told you it was her) or what has
come and gone (really. But) be
sure to say it now: what you were
wondering (at this moment) about
geese pass in frightful (regular)
intervals.

SUM

I prefer the quiet ones as they are.
Not as white fabric slipping from
sums does (not so simple). Imagine
them this way: all ears until it passes
(what could be days (before we find
her there) the geese just stop (in their
tracks (do they (?) say what you will
(what it calls for) is the way a color
would be (say yellow) on its own
(taking your breath (at this time of
day) away

I wonder (then) about the sums (&
quiet days & days (that (bring (all I
can) to (you) without (notice.

In Place(s) of Light (Suddenly)

In place(s) of light (suddenly) I
welcome the green ones (just the
cuttings please) that stretch (almost)
to the center of it all & why each day
begins this way is a mystery to me. If
one is more beautiful than the next
(if one can. Just (say: as the frost goes
(so goes France) Or. Place the light
somewhere (what it is made from)
notwithstanding.

TERMINUS

(Not enough to have chosen (just
choose (among. Choose one). She
(would have it). For a t)erminus. To.
Measure(s): the way (around. You
know. He could. Step lightly). Sort
(through casual remarks as) I knew
you would (when (if spoken to) tell
a story about us). It appears closer
to (what) she does (recognize) that
(lately it does not). Sometimes (she
said) if you stop in your tracks. Place
the loose ones in flower boxes (the
rough-edged ones). Before the stems
go numb (or worse).

AS SWEET AS SWEET ONES ARE

I know. Once (said). A man('s) sweet
ones (are). Sometimes. (Just) beyond
us. At times (like this) the color may
be (off). Or. Maybe (we just) take
it for granted. If I am in (position
(would that be enough) to keep (an
adequate distance) as (some (would
have. Surprises (even. Me).

I like the crisp ones. The sweet ones.
The ones that are (as) sweet as (the)
sweet ones are. Those. Yes. Those.

I PAINT POLKA DOTS

(for Ben)

With polka dots I paint green ones.
I paint purple polka dots madly (&
think of the things polka dots have
(call it certain presence (time to spare
(more pleasure than otherwise)

Imagine that) in the pocket of a
recent acquaintance (given (prone (?)
to (polka dots) & stories of process)
wait in height order) fall at the same
speed as paper (always) does

A(n)way (). One day (only certain
ones) come calling & leave color
everywhere (imagine the cost.

Though still) I have a yen for polka
dots (did I mention (?) I am available
for polka dots & always will be &
only later (when she asks (& she
does) about the rain (she says (give
it a name. I). Think of polka dots (I
do). By the bed stand. Let fall.

AT HOME WITH THE PICKLE FAMILY CIRCUS

It's not for nothing that the walls have ears (. Remember, your father told you so in the first instance). I mean (rather: there is plenty of room for the flies (the feathers & (do we make amends this way). Time for all that (talk) later).

THE ACROBATS (IT SEEMS

Are to blame for the sudden
downturn. The mischievous keep the
key indicators current (& downplay
the need for further action.

Some covet acrobats & (some come
early & stay through the better part
of coming weeks)

I have a house full of acrobats (I can
count (on) acrobats (to know a thing
or two about them)

Some say: let the acrobats fall where
they may or fit a fishbowl around
them. I am aware of the strain
(though) as the acrobats hover above

About these acrobats (it seems) not
much is known.

ELEMENTS. (PRESSING COINS)

I am late (the Observatory closes at 5:00 & the German girl ... (well you know how German girls are) will not wait. It is more likely that the driver understands. The turnstile is broken & barricaded with cards & transfer slips (for efficiency (economy (is all) I ask for & to) notice) the implications of: (how we ride for free will play downtown (have them photographed and processed before all else.

The buses line K Street (the farmers are next). We head to a place in the old part of town. We wait on the vintners. Small salads and omelets. Pronto. She says: I know where the fish are hiding (as we all do. If so (then) is it too much to keep inside). The waiter taps my shoulder (& sticks it to my ribs. The Observatory (it seems) was a hit with the German girl) he says)

The fires are out (in the better places) & the forecast calls for more (she no longer minces words (it is the first rule of irony: keep the elements close at hand) coins (like pressing coins (press back.

P IS (FOR) PLATTER

I show Ben a platter (for P) and A
(Bi)cycle for B. A carriage (attached
to a rail stands for R) let) loose
change (...) the primary colors. It is
a good start for one day (the rest will
come in time (though. He says) some
things (regard) their certain others as
less than a pair (are they done as they
are? It is a valid question).

Conversations in a Leap Year

In a leap year the length (of it) suffers
(is it that. Or (as) all else adjusts (does
it keep the mechanism whole.

The problem (she said) is that (unless
opportunity leaves us currently bare)
we do best with what approaches or

is likewise lost.

Not that it was (supple) once (similar
regrets torn & longer days (as a leap
year has. (But to collect them all
in one place (for her to say (about
them) that they are like (the) newer
roses) the green ones) the ones born
just yesterday). As (blue as) certain
(roses are)

simply given to conversations (about
a leap year. The how of it. When it
goes (for good.

Dial (s

o where (on his card) did it say that
his father was a diplomat (a counselor

rather) in the French sense). The
ambassador who hears footsteps all
the way from Zaire

Notice nothing out of the ordinary

By mid-morning the contagion
is isolated (they advise us to keep
close) place flower pots at the south
entrance (as the canal waters rise &
the hospital lights hold firm. The
work on the retaining walls resumes
& the mosquitoes appear to be under
control (it has been over an hour).

We are relieved at the developments
in the other sectors. The buses begin
to run again.

His father is slow to like him.
Though his birth year is a good year
for England (he says). The success is
short lived.

Does it take more than a few dollars
(he asks) to adjust the dials. I can
make a feather cap from rain. (If. The
warm weather continues (it is. Spring
after all).

EGRESS) THESE LEMONS. FOR EXAMPLE

In a word) these lemons have
fine edges (the smoke clears (wet
branches hold firm

in (manners of egress. Take the short
stick. An example of (drawn or)
otherwise drag (it against a metal
fence

emergence

TASKING BILLETS

Is it) the usual geese (they)
echo (neatly. Stacked) pieces.

Of

(hollow pipe.

One   (deserves.   Another
brings. Enough.

Big buildings (for instance

careful (as we are (to s(t)ay
fixed on: (what grain grows
here).

BREACHING THE RESERVOIR GEESE

(The swelling

Is part way through
a wooden fence

The time for an early meal
has passed

& the afternoon rush is
breeching

The reservoir geese

One by one)

HAT (DANCE

Now) if the government worker
had simply chosen an ordinary hat
the whole incident could have been
avoided

Leaving the metro she adjusts her
bag & skirt & the branches against
her waist

On the second day the hat hung over
his shoulders) water drained from its
edges

She plants annuals in his wake (&
wax beans for later)

The gullies are done for

She watches tall ships in the harbor
(waits for the fog to lift.

It is not for nothing that they pass
each year.

EVER(Y FOLD A FLOWER

There are bears in the National
Gallery again. The small ones
(cantilever (improbably) behind
the second Derain. A concession to
the park (you say (they are dressed
(for success & know the limitations
of (small bears (still (I) like the kids
who step out for Jesus (the helix
lasts (& lasts long) & if) you forget)
to include the crowd from below
the armory (uneven water pipes &
spoons in each hand) so be it. They
are (after all (under the radar (say)
famously). We could wait all day for
this float to pass. It is for ever)y fold
a flower. Once at the waist (don't
stop there) cold lemon water for
company.

To (Dispense (with) the (Crocodiles

The good ones remember to dispense
with the crocodiles (cutting through
(both) bindings of raft & lady tied
two days prior.

Initially they lay up against the
high back shoals with lady & raft
& bindings secure. As a slow rain
(hardens (&) the good ones (speed
the knife for (what (seems endless)

& granted (it comes at the last minute
(save other options (if this one fails)
& then

awake in a house on a city street of a
certain block (I am certain to return
(to it if) a slow rain gives as good as
this one (gets

to (keep us (forming...) nothing un
(due (promised here)

She says: remember the bindings
for another day & the crocodile
(dispensed with earlier) will make
good conversation later

While he asks about what (you
would say if... (though) not often
enough

THE MISSION BELLS

(for Zoe and Sophia)

The mission bells take nothing for
granted

Black hats cross McPherson Square
(eating lemon pastries as the sun
pivots & shifts in its tracks.

There is an upturn in the measures
(you say). & so) (ends (what the
indications clearly intend.

I know (some (days) look best in
winter. Covered in talc & stretched
across the bed. While lemons (keep
our wits up & up & up. If not
longing) then for the origin of (these)
things. I am certain

Is it the (waking that gets you
to remember what alone has its
pleasures in

A history of second nature

The mission bells find a long branch
in late season & come to the foot of
the stairs (before we notice. Eager to
the scent of fresh skin.

A(N)LPHABET

(for Ben)

You have these concerns

(about (a(n)lphabet: you say certain
primary letters are crooked

You say: here is

where a ball is (not) a cat is where is
the cat is not a ball

Simply stated a(n) alphabet is not all
it seems it is cracked up to be

It gives no account for the cold or
the obvious reasons for leaving

Mention the current stations (& see
if that gets you across the road with
the other chickens)

The walls hover in the various
color(s) C. The parkway is (lined
with cedars

Not that it would deter your crossing
(with more room in the outer aisles
and less space in the hips (as) I stand

The silver goes well with the rest
of her & (as they say about getting
there first: once around there is time
to go around again

I seem to have let the cat out of the
bag (keep (whole thing(s) separate
(patient as they come (calling).

SECRETS ABOUT YOU

(for Jill)

These bees want (& will) tell
secrets about you (though
(some bees) prefer to wait
until better times when the
weather turns & more bees
come calling

(that those bees would bear
these secrets when some bees
would (rest with these secrets
safe)

These bees are not shy
(though) they come on
pretense. The water pipe is
broken (the nest has fallen).
Watch for rocks & twigs &
remaining armaments. As
they (often) go unnoticed
until their lips are wet & level
with your eyes. (They

are just bees come calling
(though these bees have more
to them than that (would stay
if given the chance

& when (you ask: (these
bees) to (simply brush the

soap from your eyes (some
(I) would) love sighting them
there (at that moment. One
finger raised one bent to raise
these bees to eye level where
all things seen are tactile.

JUST GIRLS) COSTUMED AS STEVEDORES

(after a line by Flaubert)

Describe for me a line of ginger)
peppermint () absinthe in (no order
particularly l)i(ken)t(o sounds that
sound (a)like as (certain ones fall
(apart or (in the alternative) seem to
start at the)stem(the soft parts (the
(pressure these signs take (seriously)
is it enormous

or are they just girls) (put that way)
costumed as stevedores) would
know to ask (words full of scent
& (not (just) to (get on with it etc.)
(where(as fingers tire against (the
usual boxes and casings

Girls. Girls. (Girls?)

The kitchen boy lacks (instinct. I am
through (with the kitchen boy).

THE BELLY OF THE WHALE IS FULL

The belly of the whale is full

with the usual misgivings. I should
do more (he says to the Jonahs and
Sarahs and the others that (come and
go. She (has soft freckles (that come
up suddenly (on you). The walls are
covered with) missives.

BLUE

It's just a broke dump (the sign says
so (watch the sign) & what kind of
place is this anyway) for a broke
dump & a sign that says little (if
anything) about some blackbirds (&

About the Author

Born in Jerusalem and raised in Brooklyn, Tomer Inbar studied writing at Binghamton University and has an MA in Classical Japanese Literature from Cornell University and law degrees from New York University. He founded and edited *Camellia*, an experimental literary journal (1989–97), and has published translations of Saibara, a genre of Japanese folk song formalized in the Heian period. Inbar currently is an attorney at Patterson Belknap Webb & Tyler, representing charities and other nonprofit organizations, and lives in Park Slope.

CPSIA information can be obtained
at www.ICGtesting.com
Printed in the USA
LVHW11s1522111018
592608LV00004B/2/P

9 781581 771732